D1311975

SEEK & FIND IN THE BIBLE

Text by Carl Anker Mortensen
Illustrated by José Pérez Montero

Copyright © 2003, 2010 Scandinavia Publishing House
Drejervej 15,3 · DK–2400 Copenhagen NV · Denmark
Tel (+45) 3531 0330 · E-mail: jvo@scanpublishing.dk · Web: www.scanpublishing.dk

Cover design by Ben Alex
Inside design by Nils Glistrup
Illustrations copyright @ José Pérez Montero
Printed in China

ISBN 9788772477541

All rights reserved. No part of this book may be reproduced or utilized in any form or by any means,
electronic or mechanical, including photocopying, recording, or by any information storage and
retrieval system, without prior permission in writing from the Publisher.

SEEK & FIND

IN THE

BIBLE

THE OLD TESTAMENT

Text by Carl Anker Mortensen
Illustrated by José Pérez Montero

scandinavia

THE OLD TESTAMENT

CONTENTS

The story about Mini Mike is not an ordinary story. It is about a boy called Mike and what happens when he reads his Bible. His name is really not Mike. Mom calls him Michael. Teachers call him Mike, but since he's smaller than usual for a boy his age, the other kids call him Mini Mike.

Mini Mike is mischievous. He likes to hide and make other people look for him. He disappears into scenery and among crowds or wherever animals are frolicking across a landscape.

Mini Mike is a lot of fun to be with, even at home. When he reads his Bible, something special happens. The stories start to fill the room! Wider and bigger they grow. Suddenly, Mini Mike falls right down into them and then shows up in the middle of the action. In every exciting Bible story, you'll find Mini Mike looking for adventure.

But Mini Mike may be hard to find once he gets involved in what's happening. Keep a watchful eye and search carefully.

God Creates the World

God is busy creating the animals when Mike shows up. Now we're in for some fun. Mike has never even seen most of these animals. Do you recognize the one he's sitting on? What is it called? Remember, at this point in time, Mike is the only person in the whole wide world; even Adam and Eve had not yet been created when Mike arrived here.

Questions

1. Can you find the animals wearing pants?
2. Find the lions being a family.
3. Which animals are wearing hats?
4. What is the largest elephant doing?
5. How many of the animals do you recognize?
   What are they called?
   What would you call them if you were naming the animals?

Read

Genesis 1:24-25

God made the wild animals according to their kinds, the livestock according to their kinds, and all the creatures that move along the ground according to their kinds. And God saw that it was good.

– GENESIS 1:25

Noah Builds an Ark

Here is Noah. God has given him the job of building a large boat. It's called an ark. When the rain starts falling, every living being who doesn't make it into the ark will drown. It is God's punishment for those who choose not to listen to Him and follow His ways. Can you see Noah? He is trying to get two of every kind of animal into the ark. Noah's family is going to be safe on board. But where is Mike? Will he also be rescued from the flood?

Questions

1. Find Noah. What do you think he is doing?
2. How many different animals are on their way into the ark?
3. How are the parrots getting in?
4. What makes you think that Noah is expecting the rains to start soon?
5. Find Mrs. Noah. What is she afraid of?

Read

Genesis 6:13-22

I am going to bring floodwaters on the earth to destroy all life under the heavens, every creature that has breath of life in it ...
But I will establish my covenant with you, and you will enter the ark.
– GENESIS 6:17-18

Quarreling at the Tower of Babel

There are lots of people here, all gathered together in one place. Is Mike here, too? The people are trying to build a tower so high that it reaches clear up to heaven. Do you think they'll manage to finish it? This does not please God. He stops them by suddenly making them speak many different languages at one time. No one can understand what the person next to him is saying. The people can't work together on building the tower. Mike is looking for someone who speaks English. Can you find him?

Questions

1. Can you find the missing horseshoe?
2. What game do you think the children are playing with the camel?
3. Find the man with the bad foot. What happened?
4. What are they building the tower out of?
5. Guess how many persons there are in the picture. Count them one by one.
6. Can you say "Get to work!" in a foreign language?

Read

Genesis 11:1-9

Come, let us build ourselves a city, with a tower that reaches to the heavens, so that we may make a name for ourselves and not be scattered over the face of the whole earth.

– GENESIS 11:4

Israelites Cry in Egypt

These people are the people of God. They come from the land of Israel. One time when they had nothing to eat in their country, they traveled all the way to Egypt to find food. After many years in Egypt, many, many children, grandchildren and great-grandchildren were born to them. Pharaoh, the king of Egypt, made slaves out of the people of Israel. Can you see the whips he used on them? Mike is hiding from the slave masters. You probably would, too, if you were there.

Questions

1. What are the animals doing?
2. Find all the Egyptians with whips. How many are there?
3. Look for other Egyptians. What are they doing?
4. What kind of work do the women do?
5. Do the children work hard too?
6. Who is not working? Really?

Read

Exodus 1:7-14

The Israelites groaned in their slavery and cried out, and their cry for help because of their slavery went up to God.

– EXODUS 2:23

10

The Egyptians Drown

When Moses led the people of Israel out of Egypt, king Pharaoh sent the Egyptian army to bring them back. God rescued all the men, women and children by helping them cross the Red Sea through a narrow pathway of dry land. When the Egyptian army followed though, the sea walls collapsed and all the soldiers drowned, while God's people were safe on the other side. Mike is cheering for the Israelites. Can you see him?

Questions

1. Can you find the artist painting a picture? What is he painting?
2. Look for the vender. What do you think he is selling?
3. How many drowning horses can you count?
4. Find the happy Israelites. Why do you think they are so happy?
5. Look for the boy on the scooter.
6. Which way do the Israelites go now?

Read

Exodus 14:21-30

The water flowed back and covered the chariots and horsemen - the entire army of Pharaoh that had followed the Israelites into the sea. Not one of them survived.
- EXODUS 14:29

War against the Amalekites

There is a war going on here. The enemy is a tribe called the Amalekites. God's people, the people of Israel, are fighting hard. Mike wants to see who will win. He is watching the man named Moses who is holding his hands in the air. As long as Moses holds his arms up, the Israelites will keep on winning. Maybe you can guess who is helping them win.

Questions

1. Can you find the man taking a shower?
2. Find the warrior pleading for mercy for his life.
3. Find the sick-wagons.
4. Look for the fire. Do you think the tent will burn down?
5. Look for the vender. What is he selling? Is he the same man as the vender by the Red Sea?

Read

Exodus 17:8-13

As long as Moses held up his hands, the Israelites were winning, but whenever he lowered his hands, the Amalekites were winning.
- EXODUS 17:11

Eating Manna in the Desert

The Israelites are on a long journey - going home to their own country. They have been camping in tents and wandering in the desert for a long time. They've just discovered that God has provided a new kind of food for them. It is lying on the ground and looks like snow. But it's really a kind of bread called manna. Mike is finding out that it tastes good.

Questions

1. How can you tell that it is not winter?
2. Find the man with the snow-pusher. What is he doing?
3. Look for the man with skis and ski poles.
4. Find out if the animals also eat the manna.
5. How many happy people can you find?
6. When was the last time you tasted a new food?

Read

Exodus 16:12-16

Thin flakes like frost on the ground appeared on the desert floor ... Moses said to them, "It is the bread the Lord has given you to eat."
- EXODUS 16:14-15

The Fall of Jericho

The Israelites are back in Israel where they belong. This town is called Jericho. Can you see what is happening? God told His people to walk around the town for six days. Today is the seventh day. After the seventh time around, they shouted with all their might and blew loudly on their horns. When they did that, God made the big wall around the town crumble and fall down. Mike looks frightened. Is he running away?

Questions

1. How many different trumpets can you find? Can you find more than eight?
2. What else is making noise?
3. Who is walking at the front of the army?
4. Can you find any children in the crowd?
5. How many times have they walked around the walls so far?
6. Why did Jericho have a wall around it?

Read

Joshua 6:1-20

When the trumpets sounded, the people shouted, and at the sound of the trumpet, when the people gave a loud shout, the wall collapsed.

- JOSHUA 6:20

Life in Israel

Back in Israel, the people of God are living happily in freedom. This is different than living as slaves in Egypt. They love to work here, making their fields grow and bear fruit. They are working on the grape harvest now. They use huge boxes. Mike is enjoying himself. Do you like grapes, too?

Questions

1. Find the men in the huge basin. What are they doing?
2. Find some children. Are they working on the grape harvest too?
3. What kind of working animals do you find?
4. Find the man enjoying life.
5. What do you think they use the pitchers for?

Read

Joshua 24:13

When the Lord your God brings you into the land he swore to your fathers ... then when you eat and are satisfied be careful that you do not forget the Lord, who brought you out of Egypt.
- DEUTERONOMY 6:10-12

Samson's Story

These people are Philistines, the worst enemies of the Israelites. But the man standing between the columns is not a Philistine. His name is Samson. The Philistines have put his eyes out. When Samson's hair is long, as it is now, God makes him strong. Whoops, can you see Mike is sneaking away? In a moment, Samson will push the columns down so the entire building crashes down. This is Samson's way of defeating the Philistines.

Questions

1. Look for the balloon man. How many balloons do you see?
2. Find the two cameramen.
3. Locate the people hiding under a table.
4. Find the lady wearing glasses.
5. Find the man who is kneeling.
6. Have you found anyone smiling?

Read

Judges 16:23-30

Samson said to the servant who held his hand, 'Put me where I can feel the pillars that support the temple, so that I may lean against them.' Now the temple was crowded with men and women: all the rulers of the Philistines were there, and on the roof were about three thousand men and women watching Samson perform. Then Samson prayed to the Lord, 'O Sovereign Lord, remember me. O God, please strengthen me just once more ...' Then Samson reached towards the two central pillars on which the temple stood ... Then he pushed with all his might, and down came the temple on the rulers and all the people in it. Thus he killed many more when he died than while he lived.
- JUDGES 16:26-30

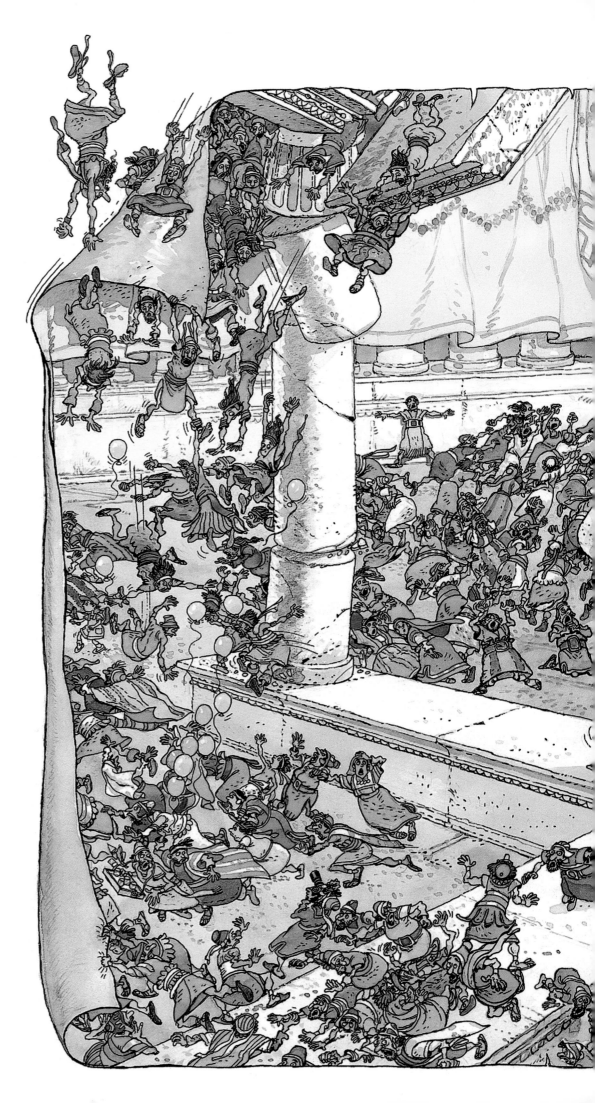

David Fights Goliath

Here lies Goliath, a giant soldier from the Philistine army! He no longer swears at God or makes jokes about David, the shepherd boy. David has killed him with a slingshot and one stone. The stone hit Goliath right in the forehead. Now the Israelites are jumping for joy and so is Mike.

Questions

1. Can you see the pile of weapons? Why do you think the Israelites left them there?
2. Why do you think one of the men is leaving the picture?
3. David is holding Goliath's sword. What do you think he will do with it?
4. How can you find out who the Israelites are?
5. Find the Philistine man biting his fingernails. What is he afraid of?

Read

1 Samuel 17:32-54

Reaching into his bag and taking out a stone, he slung it and struck the Philistine on the forehead. The stone sank into his forehead, and he fell face down on the ground. So David triumphed over the Philistine with a sling and a stone.

- 1 SAMUEL 17:49-50

David Takes the Ark of the Covenant

Mike has arrived at a party! It is a party to celebrate bringing the ark of the covenant back to Jerusalem, the capital of Israel. David is king now, he is the first one in line, dancing with joy. The pure gold ark is the most important holy thing for the Jews. It is kept in the most holy place, the temple. The Jews believed, where the ark is, God lives. Now God will be in the middle of the holy city of Jerusalem. Everyone is happy. Can you see Mike dancing, too?

Questions

1. How many different musical instruments can you find? There are eight.
2. Look for a funny bicycle.
3. Find the tourist guide.
4. What are they using for a frisbee?
5. Find the kids playing wheelbarrow.
6. Give a reason why you should dance for joy.

Read

2 Samuel 6:1-19

David danced before the Lord with all his might while he and the entire house of Israel brought up the ark of the Lord with shouts and the sound of trumpets.

- 2 SAMUEL 6:14-15

Building God's Temple

These people are building a temple. Before King David died, he had arranged for all the materials needed. His son, Solomon, is king now. God told Solomon exactly how to build the temple. It is going to be big. It's good there are many construction workers and craftsmen to do the work. Mike won't be much help. But he's going to hang around and watch.

Questions

1. Can you find workers on roller skates?
2. How many different animals are being used in the work?
3. Look for the line of workers carrying stones. How many are there?
4. How did they find out what the temple should look like?
5. Why is smoke coming out of the chimney?
6. What else was Solomon famous for?

Read

1 Kings 6

... the temple was finished in all its details according to its specifications. He had spent seven years building it.

- 1 KINGS 6:38

Jerusalem's Walls

Have you ever seen so many builders working on a project? The walls of Jerusalem have been destroyed by Israel's enemies and the gates were burned to the ground. Mike is speaking with someone. The man's name is Nehemiah. Nehemiah is directing the whole operation, rebuilding the giant walls of Jerusalem. It is important for Israel to rebuild the walls so they will be safe from their enemies.

Questions

1. Can you find the man carrying his donkey on his shoulders?
2. Where is the man on a skateboard?
3. Find a mouse.
4. Can you find the boy pulling a cat by the tail?
5. Find a kangaroo in the picture.
6. Look for the man taking a video.
7. How many different animals are you able to find? How about seven?
8. Can you point out the man with a sword in his belt?

Read

Nehemiah 6

So the wall was completed – When all our enemies heard about this and all the surrounding nations saw it, our enemies lost their self-confidence, because they realized that this work had been done with the help of our God.

- NEHEMIAH 6:15-16

THE NEW TESTAMENT

CONTENTS

The Birth of Jesus

All the people you see here come from this city - Bethlehem, except for Mini Mike - he comes from USA. Everybody is in Bethlehem to be counted and registered. Mike is here to see little Jesus. Can you find him? Mike is very excited. He is almost afraid to go any closer. Jesus is God's own Son. Mike knows that, but do you think the others know it? Where are the shepherds and their sheep?

Questions

1. Find the place where people go to be registered and counted.
2. No one has counted the sheep. How many are there?
3. Who do you think the three people riding on the camels are?
4. Where is the soldier about to lose his spear?
5. Can you see three children going very fast?

Read

Luke 2:1-18

Today in the town of David a Savior has been born to you; He is Christ the Lord. This will be a sign to you: You will find a baby wrapped in strips of cloth and lying in a manger.

-LUKE 2:11-12

The Boy Jesus at the Temple

Here we are in Jerusalem. Jesus is now twelve years old. Sometimes, like today, He is very hard to find. Joseph and Mary have finally found Jesus in the temple. Mini Mike already knew Jesus was here, so he found Him first. It is very difficult to understand what Jesus and these old, wise men are talking about. Can you find Him? Where do you think Mini Mike is?

Questions

1. How many vendors, or people selling things, can you find?
2. Do you see the boy with a fishing pole?
3. Where is the man telling the people to be quiet?
4. What is the man on the ladder doing?
5. Can you find the butterfly?

Read

Luke 2:41-49

After three days they found Him in the temple courts, sitting among the teachers, listening to them and asking them questions. Everyone who heard Him was amazed at His understanding and His answers.
-LUKE 2:46-47

The Wedding at Cana

This is quite a wedding Mike is at. No wonder they ran out of wine! And there is Jesus. He has asked the servants to pour water into the big, stone water jars. Then He has turned the water into wine. Only a couple of people know what has happened. Mike is waiting to see the surprised looks on their faces. He loves parties. He doesn't drink wine, but he would really like a coke.

Questions

1. Whose bottle has just ran out of wine?
2. Where are the two boys feeding a dog?
3. Who is on roller skates?
4. Are the bride and groom in the picture?
5. Find the servants who are about to drop something.
6. Have you seen a child riding a dog?

Read

John 2:1-11

Nearby stood six stone water jars, the kind used by the Jews for ceremonial washing, each holding from twenty to thirty gallons. Jesus said to the servants, "Fill the jars with water"; so they filled them to the brim. Then He told them, "Now draw some out and take it to the master of the banquet." They did so, and the master of the banquet tasted the water that had been turned into wine.

-JOHN 2:6-9

40

Jesus Clears the Temple

Here Mike really finds out just how brave Jesus is. "Get out of here!" He cried at the people who had turned the temple courts into a market. When Jesus started turning over the tables they could see He was serious. The temple is God's house, built for prayer. It is easy to understand why the disciples look so frightened. But they know very well that Jesus only does what God wants Him to do.

Questions

1. Where is the frightened cow trying to climb a wall?
2. Find the alarm clock.
3. Where are the doves coming from?
4. Can you see a violin?
5. Do you see a calculator?
6. How many things and animals are listed in John 2:15-16?
   See below.

Read

John 2:12-21

So He made a whip out of cords, and drove all from the temple area, both sheep and cattle. He scattered the coins of the money changers and overturned their tables. To those who sold doves He said, "Get these out of here! How dare you turn My Father's house into a market!"

-JOHN 2:15-16

Jesus Heals a Paralytic

"Just great!" Mike is mumbling to himself. He has given up trying to get any closer to Jesus. But the four men have not given up. They want their paralyzed friend to meet Jesus so that He can heal him. That is why they lowered down their friend on his mat. Some people think they have gone too far. Not Jesus. He wants to heal the man.

Questions

1. Do you see a mother holding a rattle for her baby?
2. Which musical instruments can you find?
3. Where is the woman who has lost her yarn?
4. Can you find a boy on a unicycle?
5. Find the man who is balancing on a chair.

Read

Mark 2:1-12

But that you may know that the Son of Man has authority on earth to forgive sins... "

He said to the paralytic, "I tell you, get up, take your mat and go home."
-MARK 2:10-12

44

A Sick Woman

Jesus is asking, "Who touched me?" That's why Mini Mike is hiding when Jesus turns around. Is Jesus angry? No, now He tells the woman that she is healed because she believes in Jesus. "I do, too," Mini Mike says to himself, but luckily he is not sick.

Questions

1. Where are the people standing on top of each other?
2. Can you see a boy giving money to a blind beggar?
3. Find the man doing handstands on a donkey.
4. Have you found the people standing sideways on a wall?
5. Do you see a computer?

Read

Mark 5:24-34

At once Jesus realized that power had gone out from Him. He turned around in the crowd and asked, "Who touched My clothes?"

"You see the people crowding against You," His disciples answered, "and yet You can ask, 'Who touched Me?'"

-MARK 5:30-31

Jesus Feeds the Five Thousand

Mike is thinking to himself, "Isn't this Jesus fantastic." He saw Him take the loaves and the fish into His hands and bless them. Mike was watching very carefully, but he still could not see how Jesus did it. Now all of a sudden, there is plenty of food, enough for all five thousand people.

Questions

1. Who has the most bread?
2. Two people - and a cat - have already eaten their fish, leaving only the bones, have you found them?
3. Which toys can you find?
4. Do you think people had balloons at that time?
5. Where is the photographer?
6. Where is Jesus?

Read

Mark 6:30-44

Taking the five loaves and the two fish and looking up to heaven, He gave thanks and broke the loaves. Then He gave them to His disciples to set before the people. He also divided the two fish among them all. They all ate and were satisfied, and the disciples picked up twelve basketfuls of broken pieces of bread and fish. The number of the men who had eaten was five thousand.

-MARK 6:41-44

Zaccheus the Tax Collector

Zaccheus is a rich chief tax collector, but he is a short man. Look up in the tree, there is Zaccheus. Can you see him? Mike has located him, but he can hardly see Jesus. He hears Him though. Jesus is calling, "Come down, Zaccheus, I want to visit you today." How excited Zaccheus is. Jesus is the one Person he really wants to have in his home.

Questions

1. Can you see a turtle?
2. Find the two dogs standing on their hind legs?
3. Almost everybody is looking for Jesus or on their way to see Him. Can you find any people who are busy with other things.
4. Where are the two people being carried on stretchers?

Read

Luke 19:1-10

When Jesus reached the spot, He looked up and said to him, "Zaccheus, come down immediately. I must stay at your house today."

–LUKE 19:5

52

The Triumphal Entry

Mini Mike has never seen so many people so excited. Jesus is very popular as He rides into Jerusalem on a donkey. People think He is going to become a king and Mike can hear them calling, "King of Israel!" and "Hosanna!" Mike thinks it sounds great. You can see how the crowd is waving palm branches and many have thrown carpets onto the road.

Questions

1. Find the street cleaner leaning on his broom.
2. Where is the man in a wheelchair?
3. Can you see a child waving a noisemaker?
4. Have you found the man standing on one arm?
5. Look for the closed umbrella.

Read

John 12:12-19

The next day the great crowd that had come for the Feast heard that Jesus was on His way to Jerusalem. They took palm branches and went out to meet Him, shouting, "Hosanna!"

"Blessed is He who comes in the name of the Lord!"

"Blessed is the King of Israel!"

-JOHN 12:12-13

The Apostles Heal Many

It is obvious for Mike that the disciples have received the Holy Spirit. He watches how all the people around them are being healed. That is why more and more people keep coming. The disciples are saying that it is Jesus who heals through the Holy Spirit, even though Jesus is in heaven with God. Mike thinks to himself, "That's hard to understand," but he knows deep down it is true.

Questions

1. What is the man on the table doing?
2. Where is the man who is hard of hearing?
3. Find the five people walking in single file. Why are they doing that?
4. Can you see some people who have been healed?
5. Have you noticed a very clever cat?

Read

Acts 5:12-16

As a result, people brought the sick into the streets and laid them on beds and mats so that at least Peter's shadow might fall on some of them as he passed by. Crowds gathered also from the towns around Jerusalem bringing their sick and those tormented by evil spirits, and all of them were healed.
-ACTS 5:15-16

Stephen

How wicked these people are. Stephen has just told them about Jesus, how He was killed on the cross, and now the people are stoning Stephen. Mini Mike has not told anyone that he believes in Jesus. Yet he is afraid that somebody might see him.

Questions

1. How many people are hunting Stephen down?
2. Which of them have rocks in their hands?
3. Who else besides Mini Mike do you think is on Stephen's side?
4. Find the nest with baby birds.
5. Where are the children?

Read

Acts 6:8-15 and 7:54-60

At this they covered their ears and, yelling at the top of their voices, they all rushed at him, dragged him out of the city and began to stone him.

- ACTS 7:57-58

60

The Great Multitude in White Robes

What a party! This is the best party - and the biggest - Mike has ever been to. Together with these many, many people, Mike has received a white robe. It is the wedding of the Lamb. Mike knows that the Lamb is Jesus. Everybody is crying out in a loud voice, "Hallelujah! Our Lord God Almighty reigns!" Where is Mike? He is waving his hands and cheering just like the others.

Questions

1. Find the angel with no head.
2. Which countries or places in the world do you think these people come from?
3. Where is the man with a beard and glasses?
4. Can you see a man with his right hand over his heart?
5. Do you believe we shall be wearing glasses in Heaven?

Read

Revelation 19:6-9

Let us rejoice and be glad and give Him glory! For the wedding of the Lamb has come, and His bride has made herself ready.
                                    - REVELATION 19:7

Here are some of the things Mini Mike found on his journey through the New Testament. Unfortunately, he can't remember where he found them.
Can you help him out?

Questions

Guess what this bottle contains. See if you can find it.

This bird is easy to recognize.

These two small people are far away. Do you think you can find them?

What do you think this is for?

This is a wastebasket. Can you find it?

Obviously, this foot is going somewhere. Do you know where it is?

Where did you see this flag?

Do you recognize this cat?

Where can you find this happy face?

This vase has been knocked down. What happened?

Doesn't that look like a bird? Where is it?

See if you can find this face.

This looks like it contains water. Where can you find it?

Doesn't this look like a piece of pottery? Can you find it?